Fighting Fit:

Boxing Workouts, Techniques and Sparring

Doug Werner and Alan Lachica

Start-Up Sports **#12**

Tracks Publishing
San Diego, California

Fighting Fit:

Boxing Workouts, Techniques and Sparring

Doug Werner and Alan Lachica

Start-Up Sports / Tracks Publishing
140 Brightwood Avenue
Chula Vista, CA 91910
619-476-7125 Fax 619-476-8173

Publisher's Cataloging in Publication

Werner, Doug, 1950-
    Fighting fit : boxing workouts, techniques and sparring / Doug Werner and Alan Lachica. – 1st ed.
    p. cm. – (Start-up sports ; #12)
    Includes bibliographical references and index.
    LCCN: 00-91462
    ISBN: 1-884654-02-9

    1. Boxing–Training. 2. Physical fitness.
I. Lachica, Alan. II. Title. III. Series.

GV1137.6.W47 2000   796.83
                   QBI00-500167

Dedicated
to
Lynne and Camryn Lachica

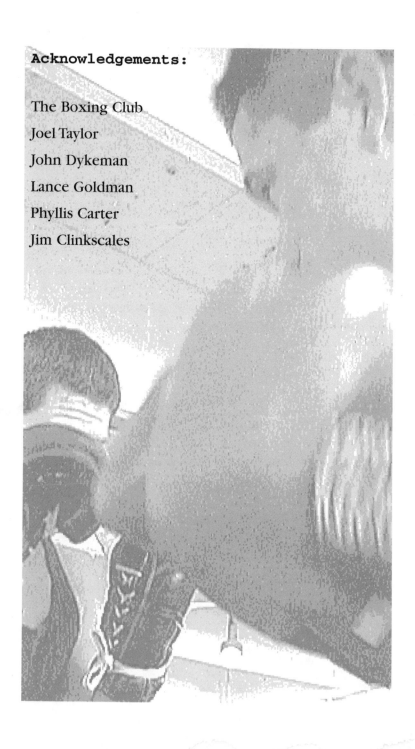

Acknowledgements:

The Boxing Club

Joel Taylor

John Dykeman

Lance Goldman

Phyllis Carter

Jim Clinkscales

Putting it on the line

Boxing has become important to me rather late in life (I took it up when I was 48!). I believe it connects to something primal, and I think many males, and perhaps a lot of females, too, share a desire that has something to do with gaining physical courage. As co-author Alan Lachica says, boxers put it on the line and there you face an array of intense emotions including fear and your physical limits. Besides that, with the right training and training attitudes, boxing can be uplifting, exhilarating and a heck of a lot of fun.

Many will turn to this book to seek fitness, and believe me, if readers take the drilling program to heart they will find it. I have never worked harder than I have sparring or even hitting the bag in earnest. Anyone who has trained seriously will tell you the same thing.

It's amusing that such a great and grand old sport like boxing should all of a sudden be trendy, but there it is. All in all that's a very good thing. Maybe when more and more folks appreciate boxing, the evils that have plagued it for so many years will be defeated.

Doug Werner

Boxing is a way to escape the daily grind. It gives me something to get excited about every time I even think of stepping into the ring. I enjoy my job as a personal trainer and coach and I enjoy the people I work with, but it's not enough … I love boxing! I love the competition and everything else that comes with putting it on the line.

There are a lot of good boxing books available. Unfortunately, most of them are too vague — offering only general advice to their readers. This book was written with a more practical approach that should help beginners as well as coaches.

Alan Lachica

Contents:

Introduction:

Fighting fit, fit to fight

In our first boxing book, *Boxer's Start-Up*, we attempted to convince the uninitiated and to teach a little boxing. We talked about a boxer's passion, about the physical and mental benefits of boxing and about the exhilaration of supervised combat. Basic punches and defenses were explored in order to give the reader a better understanding of what the sport was all about and to give him or her a start toward developing a boxer's workout program.

In *Fighting Fit*, basics are reviewed in detail and pieced together in a drilling program that develops the complete boxer. The major skills — punches, defensive moves and footwork — are honed and correlated through heavy bag drilling, controlled partner drills and situational sparring.

There are loads of photos and graphics to learn by, and just enough text to fill in the gaps. In fact, skills have never been illustrated and cataloged any better, anywhere outside of the gym. It's all here for the serious student — whether you're in it for the sport or the fitness or both.

Words of caution

Boxing can be an extraordinarily enjoyable and fulfilling pursuit, building athletic grace and skill, self-confidence and physical well-being.

We encourage readers to elevate their thoughts and train safely.

Partner drills and sparring include contact. You will get hit and you may get hurt even with the recommended protective gear.

Always wear the proper protective gear.

Drill and spar for fun, for fitness and to improve boxing skills.

Do not fight in anger, with ill will or with the intent to do harm.

Boxers in this book did not wear protective gear to better show technique and detail. **We do not advocate bag drills without wearing hand wraps and proper bag gloves. We do not advocate partner drills or sparring without each boxer wearing hand wraps, proper sparring gloves, headgear, mouthpiece and groin protector.**

It is recommended that readers serious about sparring get instruction from a coach accredited by USA Boxing, Inc., national governing body for amateur boxing in the United States. Call 719-578-4506 for information.

Part one:
Basics/ review

The Best...
Cms Trainin' - Body Drainin'
Sng Hittin' - Butt Kickin'
Workout around!

Fighting Fit: Foundations

Boxing is built on fundamentals that must be tuned and retuned constantly. In fact, every workout should include review of basic punches, defensive moves and footwork — the three major parts of boxing.

Part one reviews these parts and Part two will put them together in various drilling and sparring work-outs we call the Fighting Fit Program.

1
Gear

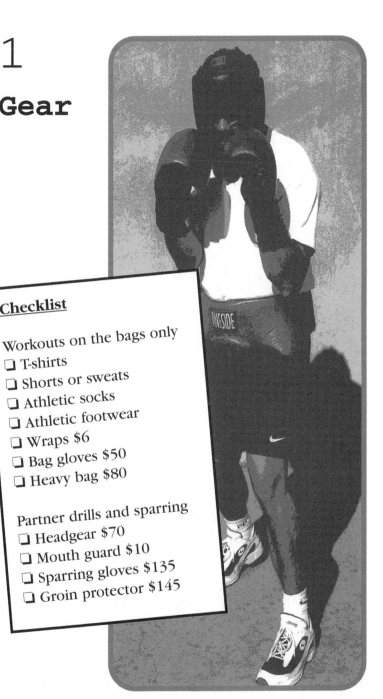

Checklist

Workouts on the bags only
❏ T-shirts
❏ Shorts or sweats
❏ Athletic socks
❏ Athletic footwear
❏ Wraps $6
❏ Bag gloves $50
❏ Heavy bag $80

Partner drills and sparring
❏ Headgear $70
❏ Mouth guard $10
❏ Sparring gloves $135
❏ Groin protector $145

Assuming you know what T-shirts, shorts and athletic socks are, we'll start with the footwear.

Athletic footwear

Sneakers that fit well are fine for now. Don't bother with actual boxing shoes. If you're training in a gym

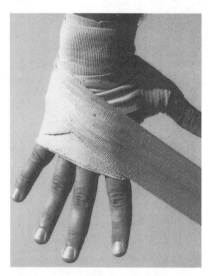

you may need to avoid dark soles that could mark up the floor. High tops are nice because of the extra support.

Wraps

Before you put on gloves you must wrap your hands for support and protection with long strips of cloth called wraps. Get the kind that have Velcro ties since they're the most convenient to use. Many fighters prefer Mexican-style wraps because they're longer and provide better protection. $6.

Bag gloves

Bag gloves are different from sparring or competition gloves. Bag gloves have just enough padding to protect a boxer's hands as he whales the heavy bag. Training or sparring gloves are more carefully designed to protect

the hands and offset the force of a blow from a sparring partner.

Bag gloves come in various weights, styles and degrees of quality and convenience. We suggest a quality pair of 12-ounce leather gloves with a wide Velcro strap closure for easy on and off. Such gloves cost about $50 or $60. The cheapest pair costs half as much, but heck, for $25 more you can get professional durability, design and safety. They're your hands, it's your choice. Like a good pair of shoes, make sure they fit and stay secure on your paws.

Heavy bag
Heavy bags come in a variety of styles, but a basic bag is about 14 inches in diameter, 42 inches high and weighs 70 pounds. They can be made of canvas, vinyl or leather. You can buy a bag with hard fill or soft fill — the

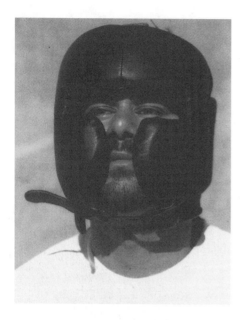

soft fill simply has a thicker foam liner. It should come with hanging chains, hooks and a swivel so it can be hung from a beam. About $80 for a canvas bag.

Headgear

Don't skimp here! Purchase a design that covers as much as possible: chin, cheeks and forehead. There are models with a face bar that protect the nose and mouth, but breathing in them is a little difficult. Get headgear with lace straps in order to keep the thing tight on your head. You don't want headgear slipping over your eyes after every punch you take. About $70.

Mouth guard

Very important unless you plan on never getting hit. The "boil and bite" variety are inexpensive (under $10) and work fine. "Boil

and bite" refers to the method used to form-fit this type of guard to your teeth. First it's boiled in water to make it pliable, then you place it in your mouth, press it with fingers to your teeth and bite down. The mouthpiece is made of material that doesn't retain heat and won't burn you.

Sparring gloves

As stated previously, sparring gloves are designed differently from bag gloves since they'll be used to strike a person and not a bag. We suggest 16 ounce gloves, padded with two inches of multilayered foam and are secured with large Velcro straps for easy on and off. About $135 for a very good pair of leather gloves. Don't skimp here either.

Groin protector

This is a girdle-like thing that protects groin, hips and kidneys. A simple jock and cup aren't quite enough protection in this sport. About $45.

Note for female boxers

Women have their own designs to choose from for groin and breast protection. Gloves are specifically manufactured for women, as well. The suggested retailers all carry gear for females and it's usually clearly presented in their catalogs.

Where to buy

We suggest you buy from a catalog because equipment sold by mass merchants is often crap. Call these respected names for a catalog of their products.

Everlast: 718-993-0100
Ringside: 1-877-4-BOXING / www.ringside.com
Title: 1-800-999-1213 / www.titleboxing.com

2

Stance, footwork & rhythm

Boxer's Stance:
Basic Position, Legs & Feet

The foundation upon which all boxing skills are based is the stance. In front of an imaginary opponent, position yourself sideways so that you present a shoulder to your target. By and large, your leading side is the opposite of your preferred hand. Lead with your left shoulder if you're right-handed or your right shoulder if you're left-handed. Your feet should be about shoulder width apart.

If you're leading with the left shoulder, place your right foot out in front of yourself so that the heel of your right foot lines up with the toe of your left.

With both heels in place, swivel your feet 45 degrees toward your target. Flex your knees and bend a bit at the hips keeping your back fairly straight. Slightly lift your back heel off the deck.

This is more or less a basic athletic posture in which you're balanced and solid on your feet. A push from any direction will not cause you to easily stumble. You are ready to move in any direction the action dictates.

Boxer's Stance: Arms, Hands & Head

Now tuck your elbows in close to your sides and raise your forearms up straight. Arrange the pillars of your arms so they protect that area of your torso that faces the target. Hold your arms with just enough tension to keep them upright. This position shouldn't be tight or rigid. Bend your head forward so that you're viewing your opponent partially through your eyebrows. At this point, your hands should be about chin to cheek level. Palms are turned in.

The boxer's stance: an athlete's ready position with hands up, chin down and elbows tucked.

This is your boxer's stance. You are equally prepared to throw punches as well as defend against them. In this ready position you are relaxed. Never tense.

Stepping

Boxing is a lot more like dancing than you might imagine. One thinks of using hands and arms when you box but not so much legs and feet. However, being able to move rapidly and economically, balanced and ready to attack or defend, is vital.

Move forward by stepping with the lead foot first. Move back by stepping with rear foot first. Seems simple enough until you scoot back and forth with the heavy bag.

Move to either side by stepping first with the foot on that side. Close the gap quickly as you step. Do not overstep or cross step. Practice by keeping up with a swinging bag.

Make quick directional changes by pivoting off the lead foot and sweeping the rear foot around it.

The idea in all movement is to maintain the integrity of your boxer's stance. Basically, that means you never overstep, cross over or bring your feet together.

There are four directions you may go: toward your opponent, back from your opponent, to the side you are mostly facing and to the side at your back.

In each direction you have a lead foot which initiates the movement and opens your stance. After the lead foot has taken a step, close the distance with your trailing foot and regain a shoulder width stance. Steps are short in length and taken close to the surface of the floor — almost in a slide.

Stepping and pivoting
with the bag.

As the bag
approaches,
step in the
new direc-
tion.

Pivot and slide
around it.

Pivot & Slide
Quick changes in
direction are made
by sweeping the
rear foot in either
direction and piv-
oting off the ball of
your lead foot.
Again, the sweeping
motion of the foot is
held close to the
floor surface.

Boxer's Rhythm
Boxers never stand
still. There should
always be some sort
of motion going on
between steps and
punches to keep
you primed,
pumped and ready
for action.

There's the long
rhythm, which is a
kind of mellow back
and forth bouncing
between the feet.
The short rhythm is
a more aggressive
side-to-side that
involves moving the
head and shoulders.

Stance, footwork & rhythm

Whether your rhythm is long (above) or short (below), head should move a head-width with every move.

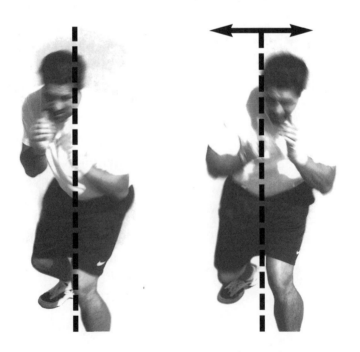

One of the all-time rivalries in boxing history show-cased the two rhythm styles: Muhammad Ali and Joe Frazer. Muhammad Ali was the classic long-rhythm guy. His game was outside fighting -- using the jab and moving around the outskirts of an opponent's range. His arch rival, Joe Frazer, was an inside fighter and the classic short-rhythm boxer. Since inside fighters are always within the striking zone of an opponent, Frazer had to keep his head moving at a brisk (almost furious) pace in order to make himself a harder target to hit.

Practice the two rhythms until they become natural and fluid -- like dancing -- and incorporate them into your drills. Remember, you don't boogie when you step or throw punches.

Getting it together in front of the mirror may take some time. Developing an inner beat is a personal thing, and combined with the stepping and punching, can be a little tricky. But keep at it. Good form goes hand in hand with technical proficiency. Getting it right will enhance your skills and looking sharp builds self-confidence.

3

Punches

Illustrations in this chapter break down and demonstrate proper technique for the major punches. This is how you should look in your training mirror. When you begin drilling and practice mirror training (Chapter 6), refer to this section to check yourself out.

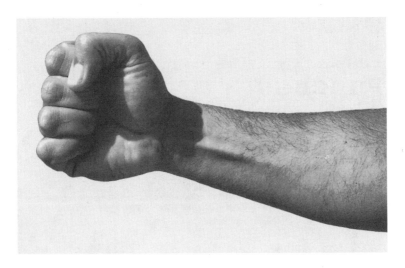

Make a fist
The thumb rests below the tucked in fingers, not curled inside, but you knew that. What you might not know is that the fist is not clenched until just before point of impact. Hands are held loose in readiness (like everything else) — even on the way to the target. Ideally the fist tightens as it lands and immediately relaxes as it's pulled back. You don't use energy until you need it. And that's a law that underlines everything you do in boxing.

Note for southpaws
For convenience, most of the book will focus on instruction for right-handed or left-foot-forward readers. If you're left-handed or prefer to box with the right foot forward, reverse the instructions where applicable.

Jab (1)
Meet the most important punch in boxing — the one you'll use the most in your boxing career, whether

you're fighting for fitness or glory.

In the boxer's stance your fists are held in a relaxed, palms-in, ready position. The jab is a punch thrown with the leading hand straight from the chin in a direct line toward your target. As the hand leaves its guard position next to your chin, the fist rotates a quarter to a half notch. As the punch is delivered, the fist gradually clenches and is completely clenched just before impact. It is then immediately relaxed and withdrawn into the guard position.

The jab is the busiest weapon in boxing because it can be thrown quickly without compromising a boxer's defensive posture. It's utilized to score, to keep opponents at bay, to set up combinations and power punches and to wear down defenses.

Although the jab is not considered a power punch, an effective use of the jab over the course of a bout will cause a considerable deal of damage. A boxer can also learn to stiffen his jab by turning his hips with the punch and stepping into its delivery.

I'm told that the jab is the only punch to use in a street fight because it can be thrown with a great deal of effectiveness without risking exposure, loss of balance or mobility. The wallop of a crisply thrown jab is more than enough to break a nose and hopefully end the dispute.

Watch any competitive bout and the jab count far exceeds that of any other punch. It's the bread and butter of offensive boxing.

The jab is an arm punch thrown directly from the chin. It's used to set up power punches and keep opponents at a distance.

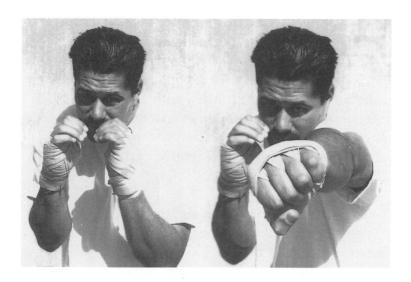

The jab does not compromise the boxer's stance or your defensive posture.

Learn to throw the jab with a step of the lead foot (below). By stepping with the jab, a boxer closes distance and is in position to use power punches.

Breathing

Exhale through pursed lips in short, spitting wheezes as you deliver all your punches. Believe it or not, the tendency is to hold your breath when punching. Perhaps it's the excitement, but at any rate, not breathing is a bad habit that should be avoided.

Jab notes

The jab is thrown directly from the chin with no wind-up or shrugging of the shoulders. The jab snaps toward its target and is pulled back immediately. A quick recovery is just as important as a quick delivery.

Straight right (2)

Your first favorite punch will be the one you throw with your preferred hand — naturally!

For the right-handed boxer, it's the straight right. From the guard position, the right hand is thrown straight from the chin on a direct line to the target. Unlike the jab, which is an arm-powered punch, the right is powered by a torquing torso and a pivoting right foot. Feel your back get into this one. The punch should accelerate and explode as the right heel of your pivoting foot swings outward. After impact the hand is sharply returned to guard.

Because of the weight transfer involved, the straight right is considered a power punch. But the weight transfer is also the weakness of power punches because for a nanosecond the boxer is without a balanced boxer's stance, and is therefore somewhat exposed. Hence the importance of getting back to guard quickly. The risk of throwing this punch too often far outweighs the natural pleasure of launching your favorite hand. The straight right is best utilized behind the jab or as a counter after a defensive move.

Right notes
The straight right should be thrown straight from the chin without wind-up or dips of the shoulder. The punch accelerates as it tracks toward the target. Immediately before the explosion the fist clenches. Tension is immediately released as the hand snaps back to guard.

Left hook (3)
The legendary left hook is the most difficult punch to learn. Unlike the jab and straight right, the left hook has mysterious nuances that simply take time for most boxers to discover and assimilate.

The hook is generally misunderstood. Most beginners think the left hook is some sort of sweeping, round-house punch thrown and powered by a loopy left arm.

The hook is an inside power punch. It's most effective when you're close to your opponent. The punch begins with a weight transfer to your left side. From the guard position the left elbow is brought up, almost parallel to the floor, so that the arm forms a sort of hook (hence the name). At the same time the fist is rotated either palm down for a very close target or palm-in for targets farther away.

Here's the secret. The arm is held in place as described above; the punch is delivered by pivoting left foot, left leg and torso sharply to the right in a powerful, one-

Punches

The straight right is powered by leg, back and shoulder. Pivot off the right foot and deliver the punch straight from the chin.

The elbow stays tucked until it moves forward with the punch — it does not draw back. No good punch is ever drawn back.

piece torquing action. The arm does not move independently of the whole. Like a gate swinging around its hinged post, this punch is powered by leg, hips, back and everything else in the barn. When it's thrown properly, it's one of the mighty weapons in boxing and is held in very high esteem.

Think about *crushing peanuts* with the ball of your left foot as you swing it around and think *Hey buddy!* as you bring the punch to completion by tucking it into your chest (like you're hugging him high around the neck). Like all punches, the hook accelerates as it tracks to the target, the fist clenches before impact and is sharply returned to the guard position along with everything else that went for the ride.

Remember, recovery is everything. Punches should never hang. Punches SNAP! Think acceleration, SNAP, recovery.

Left uppercut (5)
Uppercuts are stock and staple for inside fighting and are thrown with power coming from the legs and torso. They are not wind-up arm punches. From the guard position, dip the left shoulder so that your elbow nears your hip. At the same time rotate the fist palm up. Without cocking the arm back or winding up, propel this punch with the left side of your body. Accelerate, SNAP and recover. The right uppercut is a mirror image of the left.

Punch reminders
All punching action is best executed from a balanced boxer's stance. This ensures power, accuracy and

recovery. Punching off balance is ineffective and risks maximum exposure.

Jabs and straight rights or lefts are delivered directly from the chin with no preamble (wind-up, dips, shrugs).

All punches are SNAPPED! Accelerate, SNAP and recover. This includes sharp delivery and sharp recovery. A punch that hangs or is not recovered immediately exposes an entire half of a boxer to attack.

Guard up!
Never forget the hand that isn't punching. While one hand is attacking the other is in guard position. This is crucial — yet easy to forget! — when both hands are busy executing combinations of punches.

Intent on delivering his right hand, he nevertheless has his left hand in guard position — like it's glued there.

Punches

The left hook is powered by a fierce torquing of leg, back and shoulder over a pivoting left foot. All movement is done singularly as in one piece. The elbow is brought up to position without drawing back.

Punches

The force of an uppercut is generated by pushing off the ground on a given side and bringing hips, back, shoulder and arm up together in one violent movement.

It is particularly easy to cock the arm back for this punch. Remembering to initiate the punch by loading up on one side helps to alleviate that error.

3.1

Combinations

1/ Jab   2/ Straight right

A solid boxing offense includes an array of punches that can be effectively thrown in combination with one another. In other words, two or more punches properly delivered in a given attack are usually better than one.

Double (1-1) and triple jabs (1-1-1)
These are simply jabs thrown one after the other. Care must be taken to recover properly after each one in order to maximize power. This is an effective way to deliver a bunch of punches safely from a distance.

1-2
This is the one-two punch combo of sport literary and celluloid fame. The combination includes a jab followed

The most important punching attacks are the jab/straight right (1-2) and the jab/straight right/left hook (1-2-3).

Both combinations start with a jab to close distance and set up the head.

Both also throw the right to initiate damage.

Throwing the right causes a weight shift to the left side that sets up the left hook.

The 1-2-3 should flow powerfully and gracefully. Learning to honestly throw this combination in good form will keep you occupied for some time.

3/ Left hook

by a straight right. The classic goal is to land a clean jab at your opponent's head that lifts the chin so that you can rock it with a hard right hand.

The left jab is thrown as described (SNAP!), recovered to guard, then the straight right is immediately launched (SNAP!) and recovered to guard. Throughout the action you should feel solid over your feet. Otherwise, you're probably reaching or not recovering properly.

1-2-3
Add the left hook to the left jab and straight right combination. This is a very natural flow of punches as the

1/ Jab   2/ Straight right   3/ Left hook

Combinations should flow from one side to the other to take advantage of any weight shifts caused by power punches and to increase the number of angles and directions in your attack.

weight shifts from one foot to the other. After the jab and straight right, your weight is over the left foot creating the perfect opportunity to unload the left hook. The classic goal here is to expose the chin with the jab, tag the chin with the right and clobber the guy on the temple with the left.

Right-left-right (2-3-2)
Left-right-left (3-2-3)

These are power punch combinations utilizing the straight right and the left hook. The challenge is to coordinate the weight shifts in order to properly execute each of these torso twisting bombshells. As one punch lands, you should be weighted perfectly to

2/ Straight right 5/ Left uppercut 6/ Right uppercut

On these two pages is a six-punch combination built on the 1-2-3. After the jab/straight right/left hook comes another right, a left hook and a right hook (1-2-3-2-5-6).

throw the next one.

It's easy to turn these into arm punches when you throw them in flurries, but without the body behind them they aren't as effective. It's also difficult to maintain proper form, especially with the hook. These combinations are among an infighter's favorite weapons because the attack flies from two angles.

Return to guard
It's important to remember that after every punch the hand must return to guard. It's easy to forget in all the flailing, but without full recovery, half of your head is exposed and punches aren't so powerful. The tendency

to drop hands is directly correlated to fatigue. It's the first thing to go.

Combinations including uppercuts

Combining jabs, straight rights and left hooks with uppercuts is a dizzying feat, and absolutely devastating to an opponent because punches are coming in from all directions. It's difficult to master the flow from one punch to the other and to execute them fully and properly. It's difficult enough to master the transitions from jab to straight right to hook ... heck, it's hard enough just to learn the hook.

But practicing these combination is a great coordination drill. A good six-punch drill includes a jab, a straight right, a left uppercut, a straight right, a left hook and finally a right uppercut.

4

Defensive moves

In this chapter defensive moves are illustrated with a
partner and with the heavy bag. Alan (in white) demon-
strates all the defensive moves against punches from
Joel (in black).

Note:
Gear is not worn in order to show detail more clearly
(gloves and protective gear are big and blocky in
photos). Never box without wearing the proper sparring gear as proscribed in Chapter 1.

Boxing is 50% offense and 50% defense. That's not so easy to see when you're pounding the heavy bag all by yourself and checking out your oh-so-pretty punching technique in the mirror.

What you already know
The boxer's stance provides a great deal of protection unto itself: chin is tucked, hands are held high to protect the head, arms are arranged to protect the lower torso, feet are well apart and knees are flexed to provide a balanced and easily mobile athletic posture. With footwork and head movement added, not only can you survive an opponent's initial attack, but you'll be a hard target to hit.

Basic stuff, yet easily forgotten. How many boxers have suffered from ignoring the fundamentals? Leaving a chin exposed. Dropping the hands late in a bout. Standing stock still in an opponent's striking zone. Getting caught off balance. Or simply losing eye contact. Like they say, — *Keep the chin down and the guard up* — and you'll prevent disaster a large percentage of the time. However, boxing like a dancing turtle will not help you score or even survive for very long against a capable opponent.

Jab catching
As a jab arrives, place your right glove in front of your face with chin down. Pivot your right foot, brace the right leg and catch the jab with your glove. Make sure your chin is down so your glove bounces off your forehead and not your nose. Catch jabs as aggressively as your opponent throws them. Recover immediately.

Parries

It's not a good idea to catch a straight right. Power punches are best parried with a small slap of the left glove where the momentum can carry your opponent off balance and expose him to a counterpunch.

Parrying body shots

Punches to the body can be parried by sweeping an arm and deflecting the punch outside, while pivoting and sliding in the opposite direction of the punch.

Blocks

As a punch arrives, simply flex the knees and lower yourself so that hands automatically are raised to better protect the head. At the same time elbows and arms drop to better protect the lower body. This is not a full-on duck but a slight flexing of knees. Immediately recover to the boxer's stance.

Ducks

Ducks are executed by flexing at the knees and coming up in the opposite direction of any punch in a V movement. This should put you in position to counter into your opponent's exposed area. Don't bend at the hips and lose eye contact with your opponent. Keep hands up throughout the maneuver. Recover immediately.

Slips

Small, sideways movements of the head that dodge the bullet are called slips. It takes a keen eye to spot the incoming missile and a talented set of neck muscles to maneuver the head out of the way. Mike Tyson was a master of the slip early in his career.

A good way to practice slips is by dodging a slip bag or even the weighted end of a swinging rope, preferably in front of a mirror. With the knot or weight hung at chin level, give it a push so that it swings to and fro at your head. Practice dodging the rope using smallish, efficient "slips" of the head. Slips are neck and head propelled. They aren't ducks or shoulder dips.

Get good at this. It's one of the best ways to deal with incoming punches since the defensive intent is to avoid the attack altogether (versus a block or a catch that absorbs). The action is also relatively slight and less drastic than a duck, which of course, takes more energy and moves you out of your stance.

Defense and offense are hardly separate and distinct actions in a bout. One blends into the other or should. Each punch comes from and returns to a defensive posture. Each defensive maneuver can lead to an attack. It's a swirling, flowing thing and it takes training to react properly and quickly at the right time.

Major Defensive Points

● Keep your **eyes on your opponent.**

● Keep your **guard up.**

● Keep your **chin down.**

● **Keep moving** when you're in the strike zone.

● **Don't lunge** your punches.

● After every action **recover immediately** to guard.

● **Don't lean back** to avoid punches.

● **Give as much as you take.**

● **Don't get mad** — step back, settle down, get smart.

● Don't be predictable — **mix up your fight plan.**

Parry right against a head shot

Parries against head shots are small, sharp arm movements that firmly tap and deflect jabs and straight rights either inside or outside your opponent's body frame. Use the whole arm, not just a floppy wrist.

You can catch a jab (but not a straight right) with your right hand by bracing right hand and right leg over a pivoting right foot. This is a sharp, aggressive motion.

Opposite arm parry against a head shot

Parries are usually executed with the arm on the same side as the incoming punch. For example, Joel's left jab is best parried with Alan's right as in the photo opposite. In the photo above, Alan parries Joel's jab with his right hand. This is called an

opposite arm parry and can be dangerous because it leaves the head exposed to a straight right. In this instance, Alan needs to react quickly, perhaps with a right over Joel's jab.

Right block

Blocks work against straight punches and hooks to the head. Tuck your glove to your head and roll with the blow.

Left block

Outside slip

Slips are small lateral movements of head, neck and shoulders to avoid straight punches. The punch or swinging bag should just miss your head.

Inside slip

Slips can be worked using a heavy bag or a slip bag. Slipping outside means moving outside an opponent's body frame. Inside slips move inside the frame.

Right glove block

Glove blocks defend against uppercuts. Use a right block against a right uppercut and a left block versus a left.

Pivot right foot and brace your right leg for a right glove block ...

Left glove block

... and pivot left foot and brace left leg for a left glove block.

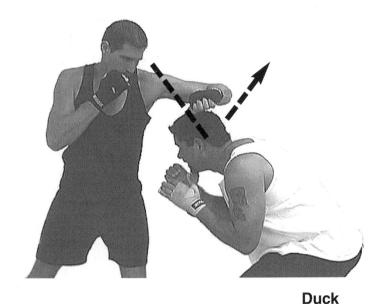

Duck

Duck head shots but never uppercuts or body shots. Flex knees, duck and recover in a **V** motion. Keep head up and eyes on your opponent. Practice with a small suspended bag.

Rock

Rocking is a sharp, balanced motion over stationary feet. Balance is maintained by rocking over flexed knees. Not to be confused with leaning, which is drawing back stiff-legged and off balance.

Step

Step back quickly with the rear foot and follow with the other in a slide.

Shoulder block

A shoulder can block a straight punch. When the lead arm drops (as to draw a punch), turn the shoulder up and into the blow.

Parry right against a body shot

Straight punches to the body can be swept to the side with a downward swing of the arm. Use a parry right against jabs and a parry left against rights. Pivot and slide away from the punch.

Parry left against a body shot

No way to effectively practice this parry on the bag.

Right forearm block against a body shot

Flex the knees to lower arms already in the guard position. Forearms should then be ready to block body shots. Turn into the blow.

Left forearm block against a body shot

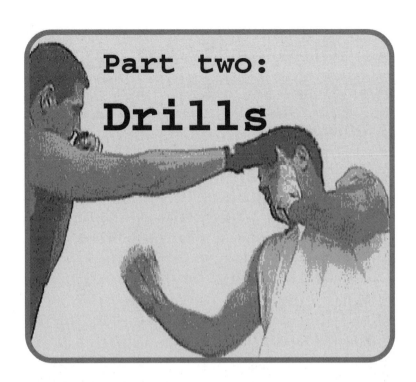

Part two:
Drills

Fighting Fit: Fit to fight

The following drills use all the pieces of boxing information that we've thrown at you so far. It's time to put them all together. These workouts make up the **Fighting Fit Program.**

Besides wraps and gloves you will need a full-length mirror and a heavy bag with plenty of room around it to exercise.

If you are serious about sparring you will need someone to spar with. It *is* possible to train on the bag alone (you will need a healthy imagination) — but nothing can replace a fighting partner.

Fighting Fit: the program

1. Mirror training
A chance to look at yourself. Rehearse footwork, punches and defensive moves in front of a mirror.

2. Heavy bag drills
First application of skills. Practice footwork, punches and combinations of punches and most of the defensive moves on the heavy bag. These workouts are each broken down into the **Five drills**.

3. Partner drills
Training with another fighting mind. With a partner carefully develop single punches, combinations and counters to punches.

4. Flow drills
Develop reactions, reflexes and muscle memory. With your partner perform a variety of continuous action drills that involve punching, defensive moves and counterpunching.

5. Situational sparring
Controlled sparring with specific goals. Work specific areas of offense and defense as well as different stylistic approaches in a sparring mode.

6. Sparring
The test and first taste. A controlled boxing match where partners perform skills in a free give-and-take at a measured pace (1/4, 1/2, 3/4, full speeds).

Build up, leave nothing behind

Training should gradually incorporate all six training exercises listed to the left. Boxers do not drop any parts of the program as they progress. Always start with mirror training and work your way to the more advanced stuff. Remember, basic fundamentals are the foundation of good boxing. Work on them every time.

If need be, **develop technical and physical skills up to six months before sparring.** Work rounds of mirror training and bag drills first.

When you know and have grooved punches, defensive moves and footwork on the bag, add partner drills to your routine. In time, you will develop enough familiarity with partner drills to add flow drills to the mix.

Sparring comes last. Your first sparring rounds should have specific training goals in mind — for example, one boxer works defense and the other offense. And sparring is not a free-for-all. Each boxer brings a plan into the ring based on training and development needs.

Three minutes on, one minute off

Drills should be performed by the round. A round of boxing is three minutes. Rounds are separated by one minute of rest. Three rounds of continuous punching is generally considered a significant workout. Building up to 6, 8, 10 and beyond rounds of working out, mark substantial gains in boxing fitness.

One day hard, one day easier

Everybody's different. Work rounds until you are tired every other day. Give yourself easier days in between.

Analyze
Correct
Perfect
Review punches, defensive moves and footwork in front of a mirror. Look at the illustrations in the previous section and get it right. Put it all together with rhythm and see how it comes off.

5 Mirror training

Look at yourself
It's very important to work punches, footwork and defense in front of a full-length reflective surface. This is the time to monitor your technique. **If it is not correct here, it will not be correct in the ring.**

Compare
Check your movements with those illustrated in Part one. Basic movements first. No punches yet. Work on footwork: front to back, side to side and pivoting. Then practice long and short rhythms. Add defensive moves: blocks, parries, slips and ducks.

Now it's time to start throwing punches. Again, your emphasis should be on technique. Get the mechanics down to the finest detail. Start with a basic jab and work up to combinations you want to improve. Work on a select few and perfect them. **Remember to mix in footwork and defense.** Establish a mental picture of your opponent — it makes your actions more purposeful.

Shadowboxing and mirror training are basically the same. Shadowboxing can also be performed in the ring or gym without the aid of a mirror.

Start slow and end fast.

6

Bag drills

Just a bag, but I love it
A heavy bag is usually made of leather, canvas or vinyl and is stuffed with old clothes and sand. It weighs about 70 pounds and must hang from something very strong and durable. There should be about six feet of space around it.

It isn't much to look at, but a boxer acquires a fondness for a big firm bag, just the same. After all, they do spend a great deal of time together.

How important is the heavy bag?
1. *It's the first thing you'll ever hit.* Where you will learn and *continue* to strengthen and sharpen punches.

2. *It's the first thing you'll ever dodge, block or keep up with.* Where you will learn and *continue* to develop defensive moves and footwork.

3. *It's the first place you'll experiment.* The bag is a boxer's *laboratory*. Each new step, punch, block and counter is dreamed up, worked out and fine tuned here.

In short, bag work develops technique, endurance, strength, balance and coordination. It's the place you begin and always return to. The bag is a boxing staple — always has been, always will be.

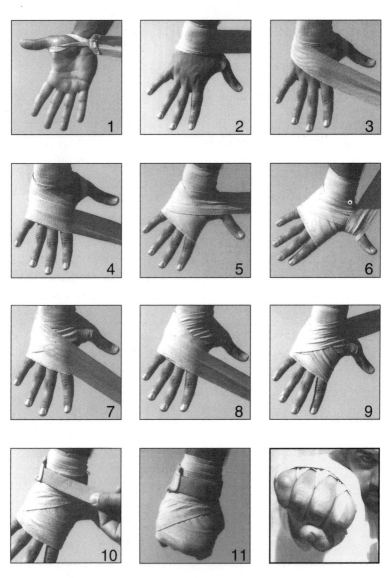

Basic wrap: Hook thumb, wrap wrist, wrap knuckles, wrap thumb, cross wrap, wrap knuckles again and tie off at wrist. Wraps protect the hands and provide a snug glove fit.

In the last photo, Alan shows a style that includes a wrap between each finger. These wraps are made between steps 6 and 7.

Preparation and ritual: wrapping your hands
First and foremost, wrapping the hands is essential to protect the many small bones that make up your paws. It is also a boxing ritual — a quiet time to center yourself, cleanse the mind of outside thoughts and concentrate on the workout to come.

Start the wrap with three or four turns on the wrist. These are fairly snug. Next, wrap around the knuckles. Wrap with fingers spread in order to prevent squeezing when you make a fist. Make four or five not-too-snug turns here. Come back down to the thumb and make a snug wrap around it. Then take the wrap up and around the opposite side of the hand and begin making an X over the hand with several not-too-snugs. As you reach the end of your wrap, bring the remainder around the wrist and tie it off. Use the kind with Velcro ties, which are the easiest and most convenient.

Another method includes wrapping between each finger after securing the thumb and before you make the X. Wrap between each finger and around the base of the thumb, then come around from the other side and cross it several times until you have just enough left to secure at the wrist. Again, make sure you wrap with your fingers spread.

Avoid wrapping so tightly that your hands crimp. It'll hurt like the devil when you start hitting the bag.

Punches, Defense, Footwork, Rhythm! Control!
Although the action revolves around punching, always
include defensive moves and footwork with your heavy
bag drills. Add blocks, parries, slips and ducks before
and after punches.

Don't just stand there!
When you aren't throwing, perform both long and
short rhythms. Control the bag by stepping and pivoting around it as it swings about.

● Remember to **wrap and glove your hands** before
hitting the bag.

● **Snap punches!** Hit the bag sharply and dead center
as it swings into your punch.

● Use straight punches when it swings toward you and
hooks when the bag moves laterally.

● Work with the movement of the bag. **Think of it as
an opponent.**

Range
Measure your distance from the bag. What style are you
working with?

An **outside** (or range) fighter's extended fist should be
about 8-10 inches from the bag.

A **counterpuncher's** about 4-6 inches.

An **infighter** will spend most of his time about an
elbow's length away.

Outside or range fighting

Counterpunching

Inside fighting

6.1 Single punches on the bag

Throw all ten when you run through the **Five drills** as described on the next page.

Jab (1) and jab body (1B)
Straight right (2) and straight right body (2B)
Left hook (3) and left hook body (3B)
Right hook (4) and right hook body (4B)
Left uppercut (5)
Right uppercut (6)

Begin with the **Technique drill** and over emphasize your form.

Depending on your fitness level and time constraints, you may want to combine some of the bag drills into one round (like the **Lightweight** and **Heavyweight drills**) — spending half the round on each.

For the **Style drill** you may want to switch styles during the same round. The Technique drill and **Bent-leg drill** should each take a full round. See Chapter 7 for bent-leg posture.

Jab

Jabs first
Snap off a jab or two at a head-high target in the middle of the bag. These jabs should crack solidly as they land and make the bag swing slightly and directly away from you without spinning.

Five drills

Beginning with single punches, run each punch and each combination of punches through these specific exercises.

1. Technique drill
Work slowly and over emphasis form on each punch.

2. Lightweight drill
Emphasize speed of movement (like a lightweight boxer).

3. Heavyweight drill
Emphasize power (like a heavyweight boxer).

4. Style drill
Practice the punches and movements that define inside fighting, outside fighting, counterpunching and in and out fighting.

Outside fighting
Makes use of a long rhythm, the jab, and plenty of footwork.

Inside fighting
Utilizes a short rhythm, lots of defense (blocks and ducks), pivoting, some side-to-side stepping and short powerful punches.

Counterpunching
Works off an opponent's punch. A boxer must imagine the punch being thrown, perform a suitable defensive move and throw a proper counter.

In and out fighting
Combines the essentials of inside and outside fighting.

5. Bent-leg drill
Throw punches with knees fully flexed. This is a lower body conditioner that develops power.

If the bag spins, you're off target. If it's really swinging you're pushing your punches. Remember, your jab should SNAP — accelerate, WHAP and recover. You almost pull the punch. There is no follow-through (as in a golf swing). The sound and feel of the punch on the bag will tell you if you're hitting properly. It's a sweet feeling — like a ball on a bat. WHAP! WHAP! WHAP!

At first, practice your jabs from a solid stance to groove your form. Throughout the punch you should be balanced and in control.

Try double and triple jabs, bringing your glove all the way back to guard after each punch. Feel that deltoid burn. Work on quickness and accuracy with and without power. Keep your right arm in tight and twist your hips a bit with the punching action to deliver stiffer jabs.

Jabbing with footwork and rhythm

After you've jabbed from a static position for a while, try incorporating movement. Step into your jab going forward and side-to-side. Shoot the jab as the left foot lands. In between punches and steps, try your boogie-woogie rhythm. Get into it. Try to blend the punches with the steps with the rhythm with the action of the bag. Find the beat in the drill.

Straight right

Strike the bag head high using the technique described previously. Punch straight from the chin off a pivoting right foot — swinging hips and back into the effort. Like all punches, think: accelerate, WHOMP! and recover. The WHOMP! indicates the deep sound of the

Straight right

harder blow — your right should really rock the bag. Remember to pull the punch upon impact in order to get that SNAP thing going and to prevent the bag from swaying wildly after each right-hand delivery.

Left hook

Left hook

You need to get in close to practice the hook. It's easier to hit the bag with the palm turned in. With your weight transferring from left to right, remember to crush the peanuts with a pivoting left foot as you swing hook, torso and hips **as a single unit** in a powerful horizontal movement. Accelerate, SNAP and recover to the balanced boxer's stance. You'll be booming the bag as you did with the right when you're throwing the hook correctly.

Remember not to wind up for a left hook. It's a compact punch thrown within the body frame powered by a twisting torso.

To practice jabs, rights and left hooks to the body, lower yourself by flexing your knees.

Uppercut

Uppercuts
Get in close to land either left or right uppercuts. Bend at the knees and explode up. Drive these punches from the hip without winding up.

6.2 Combinations on the bag
The ten major punches yield countless combinations or combos. Select only those combinations you wish to improve and eventually perfect.

We've listed ten basic combos to guide you, but strongly suggest you begin with these:

Double jab (1-1)
Jab / straight right (1-2)
Jab / straight right / left hook (1-2-3).

Break this workout into the **Five drills** as before.

Double jab (1-1)
Remember to fully recover after each blow. Try to keep power consistent from the first to the last jab in each combination.

Jab / straight right (1-2)
Don't let up or cheat on the jab just to unload on a booming right hand. Keep the jab snappy. Make sure you recover the jab fully before you throw the right.

Jab / straight right / left hook (1-2-3)
Align your right shoulder to the horizontal center of
the bag before you begin in order to properly attack
the bag from both sides.

Since the hook requires a shorter punching distance
than the jab and the right, you'll need to compromise
your boxing distance somewhat. Step in with the jab,
land a shorter right, come off the weight transfer with
a snappy left and step back out again. Don't forget to
throw a strong jab because you're anticipating the
power punches that follow. Work especially on the tran-
sition from right to left. And try not to get too frus-
trated by your sloppy left hook. Remember to bring
your hands back to your chin after every punch.
Beware of the droopy right hand. Got all that?

Ten basic combinations
Punches are cataloged and illustrated next chapter.

1. Double jab (1-1)
2. Jab / straight right (1-2)
3. Jab / jab body / straight right (1-1B-2)
4. Jab / straight right / left hook (1-2-3)
5. Jab / straight right / left hook body /
   right uppercut (1-2-3B-6)
6. Straight right / left hook / straight right body /
   left uppercut (2-3-2B-5)
7. Jab / left hook / straight right / left hook (1-3-2-3)
8. Jab / left hook body / left hook / right uppercut
   (1-3B-3-6)
9. Left hook / straight right / left uppercut / right
   hook / left hook body (3-2-5-4-3B)
10. Jab / straight right body / left hook / right hook
    body (1-2B-3-4B)

Moving with the bag

Move in, out and around the bag as you work your stuff. Use the steps and the rhythm. Learn how to move as you deliver solid blows. Keep your steps short, your stance balanced and your rhythm fluid.

6.3 Flow/rhythm drill

Anything goes! Stay relaxed and let the punches flow. Here you're trying to add the combinations (and anything else you've been working on) into a repertoire.

Beyond the heavy bag

Although the heavy bag is the most important punching bag and training tool, a well-equipped gym will have a number of different punching bags. Some bags are better for certain moves than others. The **Five drill** routine applies to every bag.

The **double end bag** is very good for honing your slipping, counterpunching, blocking and parrying skills. This bag is comprised of a hard, rubber-like ball held by elastic cords that stretch to the ceiling and floor. A boxer pulls and snaps the ball to get it going. Action is very sharp and fast. The idea is to match your moves with the blazing rubber ball.

The **slip bag** is designed for slips and ducks. This small bag swings from the ceiling. A boxer moves his head just enough to avoid being hit (as with the double end bag). You don't hit the slip bag. Work punches and defensive moves in the air.

Slip bag

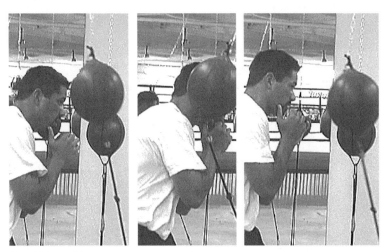

Double end bag

7

Punches on the bag

Although illustrations for punching, footwork and defensive drills using the heavy bag appear in other chapters, they are cataloged in Chapters 7, 8 and 9 for ease of reference.

You will use this section in order to simulate partner drills when you don't have a partner. In other words, you and your imagination will turn that sack of stuffing and sand into an opponent.

Jab / 1

Jab body / 1B

Note:
The bent-leg drill mentioned last chapter requires that boxers throw with legs fully flexed. The body shots of each punch illustrated in this chapter show just that (see pix 1B, 2B, 3B and 4B).

Straight right / 2

Straight right body / 2B

Left hook / 3

Left hook body / 3B

Right hook / 4

Right hook body / 4B

Left uppercut / 5

Right uppercut / 6

Since the initial target for an uppercut is always the solar plexus, there is no difference in form between an uppercut to the body or head. A boxer lands an uppercut to the head by following through.

8

Footwork
with the bag

Stepping forward and backward

As the bag swings away, step briskly after it leading with the front foot. As the bag swings back, step back leading with the rear foot.

The idea is to keep a balanced ready position — even when you are on the move. Do not overstep or cross step.

Footwork with the bag

Sidestepping

Always step first with the lead foot in that direction. In these sequences, Alan is sidestepping to follow the movement of the bag — to his right as it swings right, to his left as it swings left. The integrity of his boxer's stance is maintained throughout.

Stepping and pivoting

Pretend the bag is an opponent. As it swings toward you, step in the opposite direction and pivot off that foot to reposition yourself behind the bag.

When the bag swings back the other way, step back to your original position.

Effective stepping and pivoting enable a boxer to avoid an opponent's advance as well as set up new angles of attack.

Simple, yet important moves

At first glance these moves seem very simple ... and
taken by themselves, they are. Their simplicity does
not, however, take away from their importance. This is
how a boxer should move. Crisply and smoothly.
Always in a ready position.

Actually, moving around like this isn't so easy when
you are throwing punches and defending yourself, too.
Reason enough to practice footwork so that it becomes
second nature.

Stepping forward and backward with range
Practice stepping while maintaining distance. Move up and back so that the bag never touches an extended arm.

Alan's feet never cross or get so far apart to disrupt balance. His short, level steps move him about swiftly without a lot of up and down.

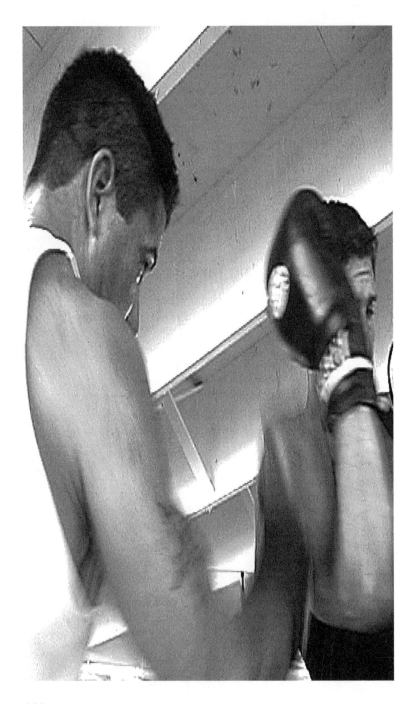

9

Defense on the bag

Although these moves are not as fun to practice as
punches, they are vitally important and should be
incorporated between each punch or combination of
punches.

Defense on the bag

Left block

Right block

Left forearm block

Right forearm block

Right glove block  Left glove block

Parry right  Parry left

Defense on the bag

Rocking back

Shoulder block

Slips

Stepping back

Duck

No slacking!
When a boxer is not throwing punches or defending against a punch he is stepping, sidestepping, pivoting or working a rhythm. You are always in motion. That's why there's a minute rest for every three minutes of action. If you're really working, you really need it!

10 Partner drills

SEE ➡ PROCESS INFO ➡ REACT

With a partner, a boxer can **SEE** the action, **PROCESS** what is going on and decide what to do, and **REACT** accordingly. As training goes on, the goal is to eliminate the **PROCESS** so that a boxer is continuously reacting to what his eyeballs are telling him.

SEE ➡ REACT

Obviously, it helps to have a partner. Sometimes all you have to do is ask the guy next to you in the gym. As you work these drills seriously, your personal boxing style will begin to emerge. Drills should be broken down each round to achieve a single goal.

10.1 Partner single punch drill

The single punch drill is where one boxer throws a single punch and the other boxer defends against it with a single defensive move. Keep your defensive moves to only a few for each workout — say, blocks versus all punches. Over time you'll work more defense into each session, but in the beginning isolate a small number of moves and groove them.

Work all ten punches [jab (1), jab body (1B), straight right (2), straight right body (2B), left hook (3), left hook body (3B), right hook (4), right hook body (4B), left uppercut (5), and right uppercut (6)] against the appropriate defensive move or moves as described and illustrated in Chapter 4.

10.1 / Sample drill / One punch (jab) versus one defensive move (jab catch or parry).

10.2 Partner combo drill

Work selected punch combinations versus appropriate defensive move or moves.

The combo drill is where one boxer throws more than one punch (in other words, a combination) and the other boxer defends against each punch with a defensive move.

Start with the basic combinations — double jab (1-1), jab / straight right (1-2) and jab / straight right / left hook (1-2-3) — with appropriate defense.

Combine different defensive moves. For example, against a double jab (1-1) you can parry right and then inside slip. You will want to work and explore all defensive possibilities, but not all at once. Isolate specific combinations and specific defense(s) against them in order to build proficiency.

10.2 / Sample drill / Combo (double jab) versus different defensive moves (parry and inside slip).

10.3 Partner counter drill

A boxer learns to throw single punches and combinations of punches. He learns to defend against single punches and combinations of punches. What comes next is the fine art of countering — hitting back after defending against a single punch or a combination of punches.

Just as every punch can be thwarted with an appropriate defensive move, there is an appropriate set of counters to use after that defensive move. Building on the same example above, if Boxer A throws a double jab, and Boxer B defends with a parry right and an inside slip, Boxer B is positioned to counter with a straight right or a left hook.

117

10.3 / Sample drill / Combo (double jab) versus
different defensive moves (parry and inside slip)
and counter (left hook).

Other possibilities are illustrated on the next several
pages. Drill the various counters carefully — select a
few for a workout and perfect the mechanics involved
in each. Start with a single counter after a single defensive move against a single punch and build up to the
combinations.

10.3.1

Countering head shots

Counters (by Alan in white) are illustrated against the jab, straight right, left hook and uppercuts, in that order.

On each of the following pages, the top photo* shows an appropriate defensive move. The photos below it show the various counters. Soak it in — this chapter shows it all: offense, defense and counters.

*Pages 142-144 show defensive moves in the first and third photos and counters in the second and fourth.

Countering a jab

Countering a jab after a parry right

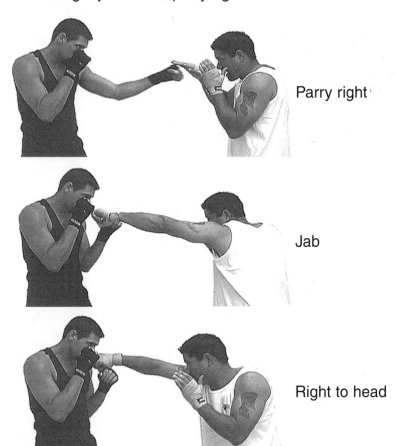

Parry right

Jab

Right to head

But I don't have a partner!
No problem. Practice the skills in these sequences
using the heavy bag. Refer to Chapters 7, 8 and 9 and
think of the heavy bag as an opponent. *Move
with it! Hit it! Block, slip or parry the imaginary
punch and throw the counter!* After a while you'll
begin to think it can actually hit back.

Countering a jab after an inside slip

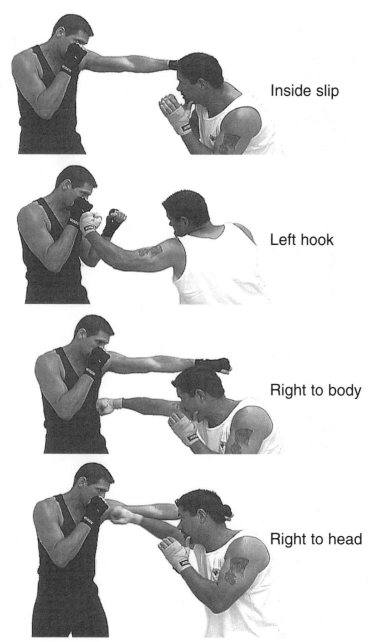

Inside slip

Left hook

Right to body

Right to head

Countering a jab after an outside slip

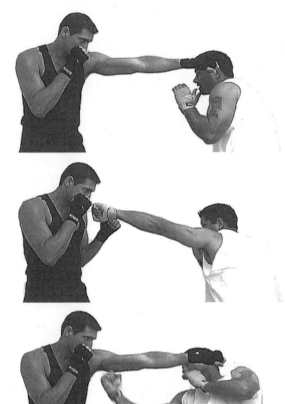

Outside slip

Jab

Right uppercut

Countering a jab while rocking back

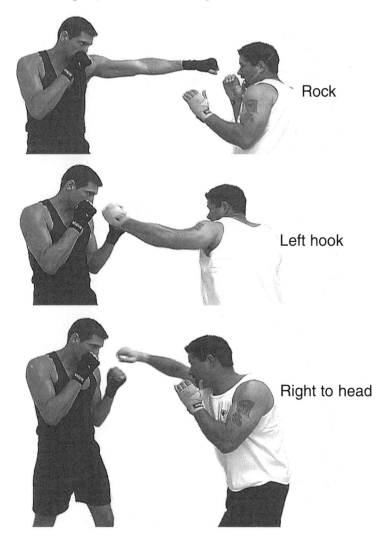

Rock

Left hook

Right to head

Countering a jab after an opposite arm parry

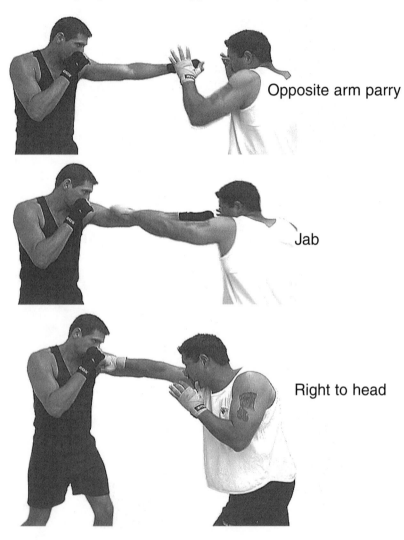

Opposite arm parry

Jab

Right to head

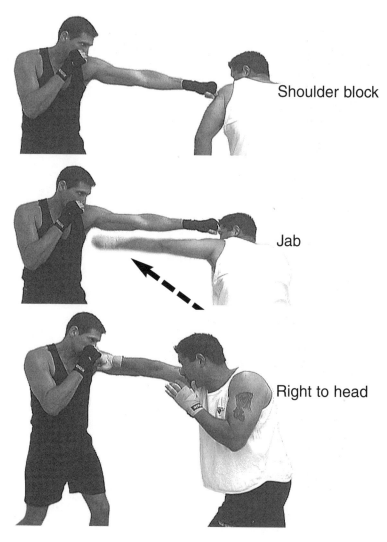

Countering a jab after a shoulder block

Shoulder block

Jab

Right to head

Countering a jab after stepping back

Step

Jab

Right to head

Countering a right

Countering a right after a parry

Parry left

Jab

Right to head

Countering a right after a block

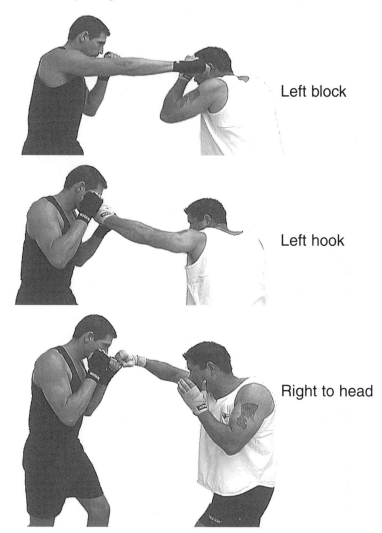

Left block

Left hook

Right to head

Countering a right after an inside slip

Inside slip

Jab to body

Jab to head

Right hook to head

Countering a right after an outside slip

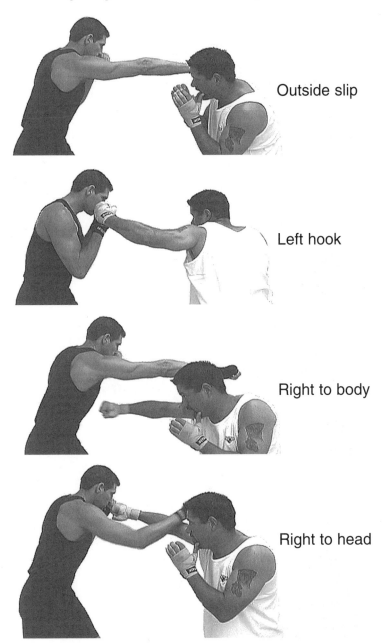

Outside slip

Left hook

Right to body

Right to head

Countering a right while rocking back

Rock

Left hook

Right uppercut

Countering a right after an opposite arm parry

Parry left

Left uppercut

Right to ...

... head

Countering a right after a shoulder block

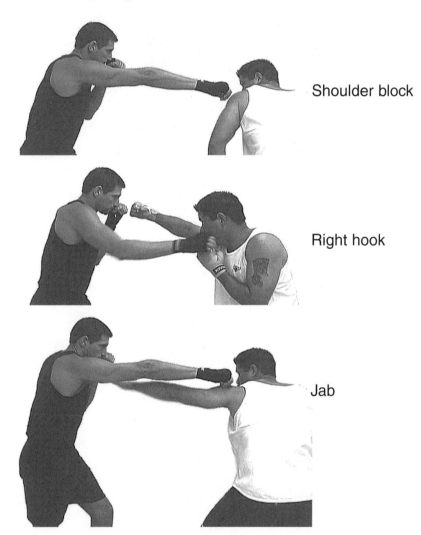

Shoulder block

Right hook

Jab

Countering a right after stepping back

Step

Jab

Right to head

Countering a left hook

Countering a left hook after a block

Right block

Left hook

Right

Countering a left hook after a duck

Duck

Left hook

Right hook

Countering a left hook while rocking back

Rock

Left hook

Right

Countering a left hook after an opposite arm parry

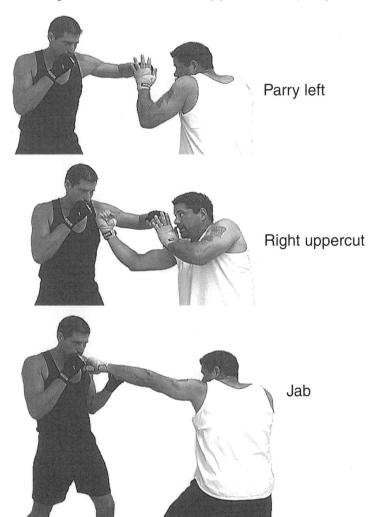

Parry left

Right uppercut

Jab

Countering a left hook after stepping back

Step

Jab

Right

Countering an uppercut

Countering a left & right uppercut after a block

Block right

Left uppercut

Block left

Right uppercut

Countering a left & right uppercut after a glove block

Left glove block

Right

Right glove block

Left hook

Countering a left & right uppercut while rocking back

Rock

Right

Rock

Left hook

Countering a left uppercut after stepping back

Step

Right

Countering a right uppercut after stepping back

Step

Jab

10.3.2

Countering
body shots

Here are the counters to the jab body, straight right body and left hook body, in that order. Again, the top illustration* on each page shows the punch and an appropriate defense (by Alan in white). The following illustrations show the various counters.

*Pages 149 and 153 show defensive moves in the first and third photos and counters in the second and fourth.

Countering a jab to body

Countering a jab to body after a parry right

Parry right

Jab

Right uppercut

After the parry, Alan will shift weight to his left side before delivering the jab or to his right to throw the right uppercut.

Countering a jab to body after a forearm block

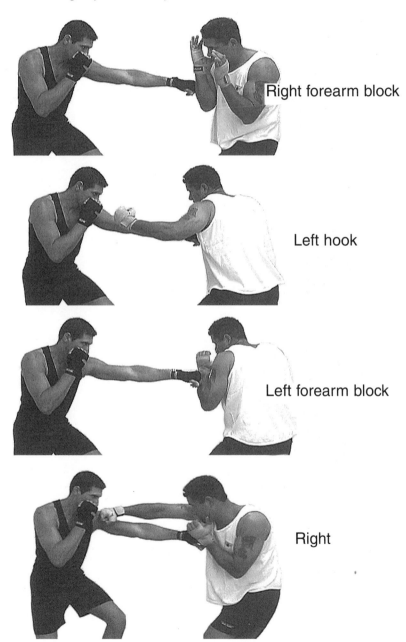

Right forearm block

Left hook

Left forearm block

Right

Countering a jab to body after stepping back

Step

Jab

Right

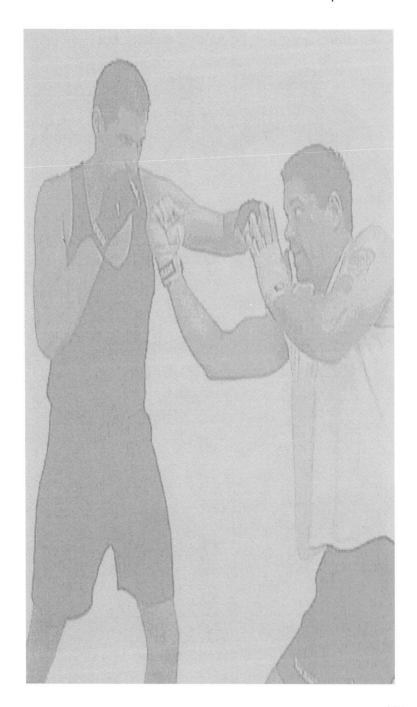

Countering a right to body

Countering a right to body after a parry left

Parry left

Right uppercut

Left uppercut

Countering a right to body after a forearm block

Left forearm block

Right hook

Right forearm block

Left hook

Countering a right to body after stepping back

Step

Jab

Right

Countering a left hook to body

Countering a left hook to body after a forearm block

Right forearm block

Right

Left hook

Right uppercut

Countering a left hook to body after stepping back

Step

Jab

Right

11

Flow drills

These drills are orchestrated exchanges between two boxers, both giving and taking through specific punches and defensive moves. Flow drills will teach you how to incorporate the offensive and defensive skills you've learned so far — especially counter punching. Flow drills are remarkably effective and exhilarating. It's the last stop before sparring.

There are ten flow drills illustrated here. Execute them in order. The easier ones are first. Build up to the more complex drills at the end. Start each drill slowly and build speed gradually.

1.1

Parry right vs. jab

1.2

Jab vs. parry right

1.3

Parry right vs. jab

2.1

Outside slip vs. jab

2.2

Straight right vs. left block

2.3

Left block vs. straight right

3.1

Inside slip vs. jab

3.2

Left hook vs. duck

3.3

Outside slip vs. straight right

4.1

Rock vs. jab

4.2

Straight right vs. outside slip

4.3

Right forearm block vs. left hook to body

5.1

Inside slip vs. straight right

5.2

Left jab vs. parry right

5.3

Right block vs. straight right

6.1

Parry right vs. straight right

6.2

Left hook vs. right block

6.3

Right block vs. left hook

7.1

Rock vs. left hook

7.2

Left hook vs. right block

7.3

Left glove block vs. left uppercut

Straight right vs. left block

8.1

Right block vs. left hook

8.2

Left uppercut vs. left glove block

8.3

Left forearm block vs. right uppercut

8.4

Left hook vs. duck

8.5

Inside slip vs. straight right

9.1

Parry right vs. jab

9.2

Jab vs. left block

9.3

Outside slip vs. straight right

9.4

Left hook vs. right block

9.5

Right block vs. left hook

9.6

Left uppercut vs. right block

9.7

Right block vs. left hook

10.1

Parry right vs. jab to body

10.2

Left uppercut vs. left glove block

10.3

Left forearm block vs. right uppercut

10.4

Right uppercut vs. left forearm block

10.5

Duck vs. right hook

10.6

Left hook to body vs. right forearm block

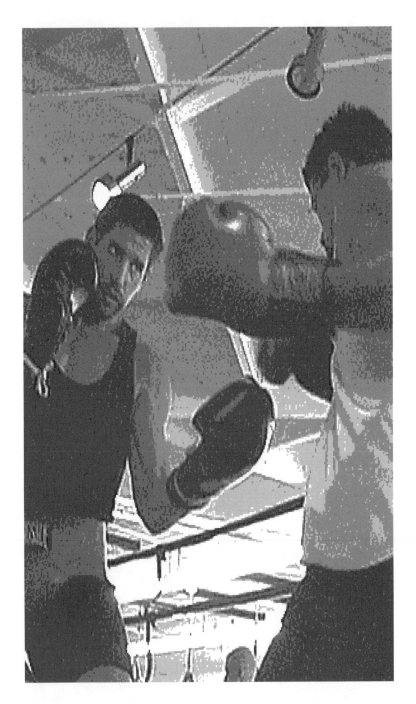

12

Situational sparring

SEE ➡ PROCESS ➡ REACT

In a sparring situation there is little or no time to think and **PROCESS** what is going on and decide what to do. In fact, it is difficult enough to simply **SEE** what is going on, even at half speed!

The idea is to develop muscle memory and reflexes through the various drills in order to reach and enter a sort of Boxer's Zone. We call that ...

SEE ➡ REACT

Situational sparring

The purpose of situational sparring is to familiarize a boxer with the different offensive and defensive fighting styles. This training will help develop reactions as well as personal style.

The more styles you know, the more weapons you'll have to use against an opponent. If you fight with only one style, you're bound to meet a boxer who can use that particular style more effectively. Better to know how to fight more than one way!

● Like the other drills, perform situational sparring in three minute rounds with a one minute rest in between.

● Always start a new drill slowly. Gradually increase speed and intensity as you gain proficiency.

● Begin with offense versus defense, then style versus style (same styles and as well as differing styles).

● Like everything else, limit what you work on each session and perfect it.

Boxing styles to learn
These are the styles you worked on the bag as part of the **Five drills.**

Outside or range fighting
Makes use of a long rhythm, the jab, and plenty of footwork.

Inside fighting or infighting
Utilizes a short rhythm, lots of defense (blocks and ducks), pivoting, some side-to-side stepping and short powerful punches.

Counterpunching
Works off an opponent's punch. A boxer must be quick to see the punch, perform a suitable defensive move and throw a proper counter.

In and out or in/out fighting
Combines the essentials of inside and outside fighting.

Range fighting
Jabbing and maintaining distance. Use of the back and forth long rhythm. Lots of footwork.

Infighting
Short powerful punches in close. Lots of sharp head and shoulder movement. Stepping and pivoting. Working the angles.

Counterpunching
Sharp defensive moves with immediate and effective return fire.

In this case, slipping the right hand and countering with an uppercut.

Getting hit

About taking a punch. Everyone has a tolerance level,
and you'll know right away where yours is. It's not a
guessing game. Some folks are OK with it and some
aren't. With head gear and 16 ounce gloves, blows to
the head should not be injurious even at full speed,
although blows to the ribs may cause bruising. Hard
punches may hurt, of course, and that's a price you pay
for entering this sport. Most of the time a punch feels
like a sharp, terrific pressure at point of impact. It's not
so much a thing of pain, but a thing of shock. At any
rate, in the universe of sport, boxing hardly stands
alone in the pain and injury department.

Flinching

Flinching is a very natural reaction when you see the
missiles approach, but a poor habit to acquire in
boxing. Work on keeping your eyes open and on your
opponent no matter what.

And flinching is more than winking eyelids. It's also

pulling punches before they reach a target when you see one coming. It's better to finish the punch since it may still land or at least disrupt the incoming punch.

Happy feet
Happy feet are common in sparring. It's fairly common to bounce backward and around and around. It's wise to block the back foot during partner drills to clip the tendency.

Hey, relax
Boxing is about relaxation and explosive action. Boxers must learn to relax between punches in order to conserve energy. Nothing takes it out of you faster than unrelieved, tense muscles over the course of a round.

Situational sparring drills
Situational sparring requires that each boxer carries out a specific role. One or both boxers may throw at will depending on the purpose of the drill.

Perform rounds of each at 1/4, 1/2, 3/4 and full speed.

12.1 Offense versus **different defenses** or styles of defense. Emphasis on offense.

12.2 Defense versus **different offenses** or styles of offense. Emphasis on defense.

12.3 Opposing styles
Outside (range) fighting verses inside fighting versus counterpunching versus in and out fighting ...

12.4 Same style
Outside (range) fighting verses outside fighting, inside fighting versus inside fighting and so on.

13 Sparring

Sparring Drills
Perform rounds at 1/4, 1/2, 3/4 and full speed.

Hard and fast
The bag doesn't punch back. A sparring partner is required for you to learn true action and reaction. Your boxing education at this stage comes hard and fast. Make sure you're ready for it and that you do it right.

Coach
The wild-ass nature of combat requires supervision. Somebody needs to control your efforts and it should be a coach. Or spar with your coach. Find a good one and listen to him. Your coach is your boxing education.

Safety first
Spar with protective gear. Spar with proper supervision. Spar with intent to learn.

Initial training
Sparring is intense. It's an adrenaline-drenched, crashing,

almost dreamlike experience. Hey, it's combat. Just you and the other guy looking for a shot. You don't think much. It's mostly action and reaction.

Your performance is a direct product of your training. It's not enough to know what to do in your head. You've got to know in your hands and legs. Hence the need for a long, sustained training period before your first bout.

Go easy

It's wise to adopt an easy-does-it approach to sparring. Learning how to hit and take hits in live action takes some getting used to. Just swinging away without purpose is no good. It won't be boxing, it won't be safe and it won't be much fun. There's simply no point to it.

Plans

Your initial sparring should be highly controlled learning sessions. You're working stuff out, not trying to beat somebody up. Go into these practice bouts with simple game plans. Work on specific things. Perhaps during one round you'd like to sharpen your jab and use a lot of slips. During another round try a lead right and certain counterpunches. Pick one or two offensive things and one or two defensive moves.

Keep it manageable in your mind. Otherwise it'll become a brawl. Why all the training if you're just going to throw it away in a free-for-all? Keep a sense of purpose at all times. You are working toward specific fitness and skill levels.

Flow

Sparring is an opportunity to try out those things you've been applying to the bag. Of course, the other guy won't be standing still because he'll have his own game plan. All those skills that looked so pretty in practice won't come off exactly as planned. Maybe they won't come off at all. You and your sparring partner will create your own little world of boxing in three-minute, action-packed chunks of time. Go with the flow.

Composure

It takes time to accept getting hit. At first you may get mad and want revenge at any cost, but that's not the point. Better to figure out why you got hit (there's always a reason) and improve upon the weakness in your defense. Your anger will impede your growth as a boxer. Composure is absolutely crucial at all times and the key to success. Even more so when your nose throbs and your pride is pounded.

Review

Watching videos of your performances will enhance your education immeasurably. Seeing is believing. See how your guard drops. See how awful your footwork is. See how slow your reactions are. When you're mixing it up it's hard to tell what's going on. You can get the wrong idea. But the clips will be true.

Common problems

● Squaring off to an opponent (planting your feet directly in front of an opponent so that you face him with your chest). Never compromise your basic defensive posture.

● Signaling intentions with shoulders, head or flying elbow before a punch is thrown. Deliver your punches crisply and cleanly. Straight punches fire directly from chin to target.

● Predictability with movements or offensive and defensive style. A boxer must mix up his approach so that his opponent won't see patterns.

● Reaching and pawing. These are largely useless actions that will expose you to dangerous counters.

● Hesitation. Finish your punches. They may land or disrupt the counter. Half a punch is worthless.

● Flinching. Learn to keep your eyes on your opponent — even under fire!

● Fatigue. It takes time and training to build stamina.

● Slow and sloppy technique. It also takes time and training to groove offensive and defensive actions.

● Nervous prancing and bouncing. Happy feet happen naturally and must be curbed to conserve energy.

● Inability to relax between actions. The intensity of sparring makes it hard to relax out there, but relax you must, in order to conserve energy and to execute technique properly.

● Anger. Has no place in sparring.

● Charging. Usually the result of frustration. With an experienced opponent you'll be cut down in no time.

Last word: Alan Lachica on sparring

● Spar because you want to improve skills, have fun and, of course, be successful. Your intent should never be to hurt someone. It's hard enough as it is.

● Realistic expectations of your performance are important. Mistakes (many of them) will happen. Reward your effort and correct technique.

● Get comfortable with the idea of getting hit and hitting someone early on. It's easier said than done!

● Get familiar with the ring (surface, ropes and size).

● Know the style you want to start with. It may change according to your opponent, but try to stick with it for a while.

● Make sure your partner knows the plan and pace of your sparring workout. We recommend that beginners spar in the 1/4 to 1/2 speed range.

● Establish a pace that benefits you. Don't throw punches carelessly — you'll only punch yourself out.

● We recommend you jab and keep a good distance from your opponent so that you can study him. Notice his tendencies when you jab and feint (hand, head and shoulder movements as if to punch). If your opponent reacts with the same move two or three times in a row, it's probably a habit — then you can capitalize on them.

● Stay under control and relaxed. Remember, there's no shame in stopping the action if you feel yourself getting overwhelmed.

14

Resistance training

Resistance training

Resistance training programs vary. However, there are certain exercises that better develop athletic movement. This program is intended to add strength and definition, not bulk.

A good rule of thumb: is when you can perform 15 reps in any exercise, it's time to increase the weight 5-10 pounds.

Total body lifts

The benefits of these lifts transfer directly to the ring. In developing skills such as punching and slipping, boxers must generate a tremendous amount of force in a very short time. This is done by using the ground to generate power through the ankle, knee, and hip joints. Body lifts develop just that. We recommend that you do these lifts 2-3 times each week.

1. High pulls	3 sets	12-10-8 reps
2. Power clean	3 sets	12-10-8 reps
3. Split jerks	3 sets	12-10-8 reps

Here are some general exercises you should perform 2-3 times each week.

Upper body

1. Chest press	2-3 sets	15-10-8 reps
2. Incline dumbbell flies	2-3 sets	12-10-8 reps
3. Straight arm pullovers	2-3 sets	12-10-8 reps
4. Bent over rows	2-3 sets	12-10-8 reps
5. Dumbbell curls	2 sets	12-10 reps
6. French curls	2 sets	15-12 reps

Lower body

1. Lunges	2-3 sets 15-12-10 reps
2. Leg curls	2 sets 15-12 reps
3. Leg extensions	2 sets 15-12 reps

Abs and lower back

1. Bent-leg lifts	2 sets 20-30 reps
2. Seated dead lifts	2 sets 12-10 reps
3. Crunches	2 sets 20-30 reps
4. Side crunches	2 sets 20-30 reps

The following pages detail each of these training exercises.

High pulls

1. Feet shoulder width, toes straight, knees over bar.

2. Grip bar just outside knees.

3. Lock in lower back.

4. Head up, eyes straight.

5. Spread chest.

6. Keep weight evenly distributed on feet.

7. Shoulders over toes.

8. Lift weight smoothly to just below knees.

9. Roll hips, straighten knees.

10. Move to balls of feet and lift bar to upper chest — elbows to ears. Weight should be at upper chest when you are on balls of feet.

High pulls

Power clean

1. Same stance as high pulls.

2. Lift bar smoothly (don't jerk) to just below knees using legs. Knees, hips and shoulders move upward together. Bar moves at rate of hip. Always keep shoulders above hips.

3. Keep bar close to body and move bar in straight line from floor.

4. Shrug and lift elbows high to ears. Straighten legs at knee. Stand on toes.

5. Explode hips inward (roll).

6. Head is up (don't dip head before clean or before lift from floor).

7. Spread feet and re-bend knee at catch phase.

8. Clean weight by throwing elbows forward.

9. Set weight on floor by bending at knees and hips (don't bend at back).

Power cleans

Split jerks

1. Start with feet 12 inches apart.

2. Hold bar just outside shoulder width with bar resting on deltoids.

3. Dip 6-8 inches bending at knee in 1/4 squat.

4. Reverse direction and explode ankles, knees and hips.

5. Drive bar upward over head with chest and shoul ders. Be careful not to catch face.

6. Split front leg and back leg about two feet from front heel to back toe.

7. Stomp as you land on front foot with knee bent over ankle and weight on ball of back foot. Feet should hit floor and elbows lock at same time. Lock bar over head behind ear.

Alternate lead foot with different sets.

Split jerks

Chest press

Incline dumbbell flies

Straight arm pullovers

Bent over rows

Dumbbell curls

French curls

Lunges

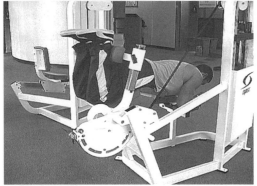

Leg curls

Leg extensions

Bent-leg lifts

Seated dead lifts

Crunches

Side crunches

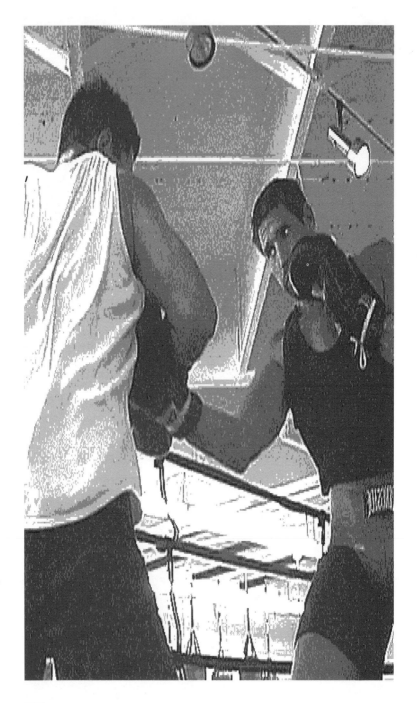

15

Stretches

Stretching

Any well planned exercise program starts with a stretching segment. Flexibility will increase naturally when you stretch, limiting chance of injury. Here are some basic stretches you should include in your routine. All stretches should be held for 10–15 seconds with no bouncing. Induce mild tension and breathe deeply throughout each stretch.

1. Seated hamstring and lower back
2. Seated quadricep
3. Seated inner/upper thigh
4. Hip flexor
5. Standing calf and achilles'
6. Middle and upper back
7. Standing chest
8. Standing deltoid and bicep
9. Standing tricep
10. Neck
11. Wrist and forearm

Seated hamstring
and lower back

Seated quadricep

Seated inner/upper thigh

Hip flexor

Standing calf   Standing achilles'

Middle and upper back

Standing chest

Standing deltoid and bicep

Standing tricep

Stretches

Neck

Wrist and forearm

16

Cardiovascular training

Although in boxing it's commonly referred to as road-work, cardiovascular training can take many forms. Whether working on a Stairmaster, recumbent bike or actually taking it to the road, the key is to make sure you're in your cardiovascular target zone.

Each person has a cardiovascular target zone within which physical activity must be maintained in order to build cardiovascular fitness. To reach this zone you must maintain 60–80% of your maximal heart rate for at least 20–30 minutes per workout.

A simple way to determine your target zone is to subtract your age from 220 and multiply the difference by .60 and .80. The lower number gives you a target for an easy day. The higher number is your target for a hard training day.

To determine heart rate at any given time, take your pulse for ten seconds and multiply that count by six.

One breath, one sentence method
A rough but effective way to reach your target zone is to exercise until you cannot speak a complete sentence without taking a breath. If you can recite the sentence without doing so you are not there yet. If you cannot say the sentence without stopping twice for air, you are

out of your target zone.

We recommend you train at the high end of your target zone 3-4 times a week.

Cool down
Once you've completed your workout, spend about five minutes doing light stretches and taking deep breaths. Get out of your wet clothes and towel off.

Glossary

Arm punch: A punch thrown from the shoulder only, without help from the legs or torso.

Bag gloves: Boxing gloves designed to hit punching bags. Usually have a flat striking surface.

Bent-leg drill: A bag exercise where a boxer throws punches with knees fully flexed.

Block: Usually refers to the type of arm block a boxer uses to protect his head.

Counterpunching: Punching into the exposed or unguarded area an opponent leaves as he punches.

Duck: Moving under a punch by bending at the knees and coming back up in the direction of the punch in a **V** motion.

Double end bag: Type of punching bag suspended between floor and ceiling with elastic cords.

Flow drills: Continuous action partner drills. Boxers throw and defend against each other according to a planned exercise.

Forearm block: Type of block used to stop body punches.

Glove block: Type of block used to stop an uppercut.

Heavy bag: A large punching bag either suspended from above or attached to a heavy foundation.

Heavyweight drill: Type of drill where a boxer exercises like a heavyweight boxer with emphasis on power.

Inside: Refers to either 1) that area inside a boxer's striking zone or 2) that zone within a boxer's frame.

Inside fighting: Boxing within the striking zone. Usually entails furious offensive action with short punches and side-to-side head motion. Also infighting.

In/out fighting: A boxing style that utilizes the characteristics of inside and outside fighting.

Jab (1): Punch thrown with the leading hand. This is a straight shot from the chin powered by the arm and sometimes the hips. The busiest punch in boxing.

Lightweight drill: Type of drill where a boxer exercises like a lightweight boxer with emphasis on speed of movement.

Left hook (3): A power punch thrown with a hooked left arm powered by leg and torso.

Long rhythm: An easy back and forth motion between the feet.

Mirror training: Drilling punches, defensive moves and footwork in front of a mirror.

One-two (1-2): The jab (1) and straight right (2) combination.

One-two-three (1-2-3): The jab (1), straight right (2) and left hook (3) combination.

Outside: Refers to either 1) that area outside a boxer's striking zone or 2) that zone outside a boxer's frame.

Outside fighting: Boxing outside the striking zone. Usually entails active footwork and jabs. Also range fighting.

Parries: Arm and hand movements executed to redirect incoming punches.

Partner drills: Exercises between boxers that develop specific punches and defensive moves.

Power punch: Any punch powered by legs and torso.

Reaction punches: Punches thrown in immediate reaction to an opponent's punch and into the exposed or unguarded area an opponent leaves as he punches.

Right-left (2-3): The straight right (2) and left hook (3) combination.

Round: The three-minute periods that make up a bout.

Shadowboxing: A training exercise where a boxer practices and perfects technique on his own, usually in front of a mirror.

Short rhythm: The busy side-to-side head motion that accompanies inside fighting or infighting.

Shoulder block: A defensive move where a boxer throws his shoulder into the path of a straight punch to the head.

Situational sparring: Controlled sparring between boxers. Each plays a specific offensive, defensive or style role.

Slips: Slight movements of the head and neck to avoid punches.

Slip bag: Small swinging bag hung from the ceiling and used to practice slips.

Sparring: Practice boxing. Closely supervised training bouts between fighters often designed to develop specific areas of technical proficiency.

Sparring gloves: Specially designed and padded boxing gloves used for sparring.

Squaring off: Coming out of the sideways boxer's stance and facing an opponent with an open chest.

Straight right (2): A power punch thrown with a straight hand powered by leg and torso.

Style drill: Type of drill where a boxer emulates the characteristics of different boxing styles — usually those of outside fighting, infighting, counterpunching and in/out fighting.

Technique drill: Type of drill where a boxer emphasizes offensive and/or defensive form.

Uppercut (left uppercut-5, right uppercut-6): A power punch thrown up from the waist powered by legs and torso.

Wraps: The long strips of cloth used to wrap and protect the hands before putting on boxing gloves.

Resources

EQUIPMENT
Your local sporting goods store or outlet will have stuff, but I suggest you buy directly from one of the top manufacturers.

Everlast
718-993-0100

Ringside
1-877-4-BOXING
www.ringside.com

Title
1-800-999-1213
www.titleboxing.com

MAGAZINES
The Boxing Record Book
Fight Fax, Inc.
PO Box 896
Sicklerville, NJ 08081-0896
609-782-8868

Boxing USA
United States Amateur Boxing, Inc. (USA Boxing)
One Olympic Plaza
Colorado Springs, CO 80909
719-578-4506

Boxing (year)
KO Magazine
Ring
Ring Boxing Almanac and Book of Facts
Ring Extra
Ring Presents
World Boxing
All the above are published by London Publishing Company

7002 West Butler Pike
Ambler, PA 19002-5147
215-643-6385

Hispanics in Boxing
R. Paniagua, Incorporated
155 East 42nd Street
Suite 206
New York, NY 10017-5618
212-983-4444

International Boxing Digest (Boxing Illustrated)
International Sports Ltd.
530 Fifth Avenue
Suite 430
New York, NY 10036
212-730-1374

Ring Rhetoric
American Association for the Improvement of Boxing
86 Fletcher Avenue
Mount Vernon, NY 10552-3319
914-664-4571

MOVIES
That Hollywood has had a strong interest in boxing over the years shouldn't be surprising. The sport brings it all to the table: violent conflict, courage, redemption, individual struggle, good guys, bad guys ... the whole enchilada. Since 1922 over 130 films have been made about boxing. Here's a small, yet sparkling, sampling that spans six decades. Note that they feature some of Hollywood's greatest stars.

Gentleman Jim (1942)
Errol Flynn

Body and Soul (1947)
John Garfield

Champion (1949)
Kirk Douglas

The Set-Up (1949)
Robert Ryan

Somebody Up There Likes Me (1956) Paul Newman

Requiem for a Heavyweight (1962) Anthony Quinn

Rocky (1976)
Sylvester Stallone

Raging Bull (1980)
Robert DeNiro

The Boxer (1998)
Daniel Day-Lewis

MUSEUMS
International Boxing Hall of Fame
Hall of Fame Drive
PO Box 425
Canastota, NY 13032
315-697-7095
Fax 315-697-5356

ORGANIZATIONS
Amateur
Golden Gloves Association
of America
1503 Linda Lane
Hutchinson, KS 67502

615-522-5885
Fax 615-544-3829

International Amateur
Boxing Association
135 Westervelt Place
Creskill, NJ 07626
201-567-3117

Knights Boxing
Team International
2350 Ventura Road
Smyrna, GA 30080-1327
770-432-3632
Fax 770-528-2132

United States Amateur
Boxing, Inc. (USA Boxing)
One Olympic Plaza
Colorado Springs, CO 80909
719-578-4506
Fax: 719-632-3426
usaboxing@aol.com

Professional
International Boxing
Federation (IBF)
134 Evergreen Place, 9th Floor
East Orange, NJ 07018
201-414-0300

North American
Boxing Federation
14340 Sundance Drive
Reno, NV 89511
702-853-1236
Fax 702-853-1724

World Boxing
Association (WBA)

www.wbaonline.com

World Boxing Council (WBC)
Genova 33, Oficina 503
Colonia Juarez
Cuauhtemoc
06600 Mexico City, DF, Mexico

World Boxing
Organization (WBO)
412 Colorado Avenue
Aurora, IL 60506
630-897-4765
Fax 630-897-1134

Other boxing organizations
American Association
for the Improvement of Boxing
36 Fletcher Avenue
Mount Vernon, NY 10552
914-664-4571

International Boxing
Writers Association
50 Mary Street
Tappan, NY 10983
914-359-6334

International Veteran
Boxers Association
35 Brady Avenue
New Rochelle, NY 10805
914-235-6820
Fax 914-654-9785

TELEVISION
There's lots of boxing on the
tube. Check your listings. By the
way, when television first
began, boxing was one of its
biggest draws. Boxing could be

seen every night of the week
during the 1950s and its ratings
rivaled those of *I Love Lucy.*

These networks and programs
provide the action as this book
goes to print:

ESPN

ESPN2
Especially notable about ESPN2
are the *Friday Night Fights.* This
show features good fighters,
great commentary (Teddy Atlas
will teach you something new
each week), boxing news and
clips of historic boxing
matches. Great stuff!

Fox Sport Network

HBO's Boxing After Dark

Pay-Per-View

Showtime Feature Events

USA's Tuesday Night Fights

VIDEOS
Blockbuster
Look in the sports or special
interest sections. You may be
surprised. In my local outlet I
found six hard-core boxing
videos including tapes on Julio
Caesar Chavez, Mike Tyson,
Muhammad Ali and Sugar Ray
Robinson.

Ringside
They have all the boxing videos known to man. Check out their catalog: 913-888-1719.

WEB SITES
Amateur boxing news
http://www.usaboxing.org
USA Boxing is the national governing body for amateur boxing in the United States.

International Boxing Hall of Fame
http://www.ibhof.com/

News, articles, schedules and more.
http://www.boxinginsider.com

http://www.boxingline.com

http://espn.go.com/boxing

http://www.fightnews.com

http://www.hbo.com/boxing

http://www.houseofboxing.com

http://www.showtimeonline.com/scboxing/

http://www.toprank.com/

Women's boxing
http://www.femboxer.com/

WHERE TO LEARN
Check out the yellow pages under boxing for the gym nearest you. If nothing else, you'll get a salty dose of reality. However, the sport also lurks in malls and uptown fitness centers these days, so give them a try, too. For further help and recommendations call:

USA Boxing: 719-578-4506.

Bibliography

Brown, John. *Boxing Manual*. Lenexa, Kansas.: Ringside, Inc., 1996.

DePasquale, Peter. *The Boxer's Workout*. Brooklyn, New York.: Fighting Fit Inc., 1988.

Grombach, V. John. *The Saga of Sock*. New York, New York.: A. S. Barns and Company, 1949.

Ringside Products. *Ringside Training Video*. Lenexa, Kansas.: Ringside, Inc., 1996.

The New Yorker. New York, New York: The Conde Nast Publications.

USA Boxing. *Coaching Olympic Style Boxing*. Carmel, Indiana.: Cooper Publishing Group LLC, 1995.

Ward, Douglas. *Ringside Report*. Lenexa, Kansas.: Ringside, Inc.

Index

Munns

About the author

Doug Werner is the author of the internationally acclaimed Start-Up Sports series. In previous lifetimes he graduated with a fine arts degree from Cal State Long Beach, built an ad agency and founded a graphics firm. In 1994 he established Tracks Publishing.

Werner lives with his wife Kathleen and daughter Joy in San Diego, California — one of the major sport fun-zones on the planet.

About the author/coach

Alan Lachica is a certified USA Amateur Boxing coach, the former owner and operator of Cross Boxing in San Diego and a former amateur boxer — winning over 90% of his competitive bouts. His boxing exhibitions have been featured on local and national television, including *Eye on America* (CBS News).

Lachica is also a certified personal trainer. His clients have included top professional athletes in Major League Baseball and the National Football League. He is a graduate of Cal State Long Beach and currently lives in La Jolla, California with wife Lynn and daughter Camryn.

www.startupsports.com